Maybe I Should Fly

Maybe I Should Fly

poems

Shafiqa Labib and Farida Labib

GRAYSON BOOKS
West Hartford, Connecticut
graysonbooks.com

to our kind mother, who empowered us
to reflect her and other women's emotions

"If we have no peace, it is because we
have forgotten that we belong to each other."

—Mother Teresa

Contents

DON'T BE AFRAID

Foreword

I began mentoring Afghan Women writers in 2013, through the Afghan Women's Writing Project (AWWP), founded in 2009 with the mission of supporting the voices of women and the belief that to tell one's story is a human right. The aim of the organization is to nurture, educate, and carry the voices of Afghanistan's women to the world, while offering readers unique insights into Afghan culture. Not only were Afghan women hidden beneath *burqas*, but their stories were silenced as well.

These women took a leap of faith and risked their lives to write. Telling their stories was a revolutionary act. In spite of fear for their safety, these brave women were not just whispering on the page; they were shouting truths, reaching out to the world to tell of the injustices, fighting for their lives and the lives of their sisters. Their poems and stories were published on the AWWP website, accessible to all. They had hope in knowing that "there are some beautiful minds on the other side of the world who are concerned about us." We are all citizens of planet earth.

Today, because of the return of the Taliban, Afghan women are again voiceless. All that remains for them is hope. Their struggles are not unique; they concern us all. Knowing that "history is changed by the small actions of ordinary people," I have asked myself: what could I—one person—do now to help these brave and beautiful women?

I am privileged to have had the opportunity to mentor Shafiqa and Farida Labib, beautiful and accomplished young women, as they share their stories through their poems, showing the power of poetry in overcoming oppression and acting as a part of Poetry of Witness. Through this experience, I gained as much as I gave.

Shafiqa's strong use of imagery speaks to all the senses to bring the reader into her poems and experience the passion with which she writes. Each poem keeps the reader spellbound, leaving us to think beyond the last line. What she wants is what we all want, "to find the spot where I belong." Her poems of determination demand to be heard. She writes, "Our patience is our strength," and

> "We will wash away from the black
> pages of this country all the pains of yesterday.
> Singing, we will sign our names on the heart of history."

Farida, through her beautiful and passionate language, poses questions to herself, and to the reader—questions we all must answer. She writes:

> "Sometimes, while out searching for myself
> in the chaos of my mind,
> I sink into an ocean of thoughts—
> past, present, future swirling—
> a question echoing in my ear:
> *Who am I, who am I?*"

She writes: "I am tired of dreams too heavy to carry." In poems of longing and of hope she expresses her desire for the simple things: "I want to be born again, in a place where there is peace...I want to be a poet, disappearing in a world of words."

Through their heartfelt poetry, Shafiqa and Farida Labib educate us, their readers. They write about their pain, their struggles, and the struggle of their sisters, not only as women living in Afghanistan under the threat of the Taliban, but on behalf of all women who are denied the right to feel the transformative power of self-expression. They do not waver in the face of oppression. They believe in themselves. They are global change makers. They know that when a girl is empowered, her family and community thrive. When a girl's family and community thrive, the world is changed.

Mentoring these young women has been a very humbling experience for me. I have learned from them at every turn. I have been reminded of the power of hope. The power of forgiveness. The power of perseverance. The power of love, of gratitude, and of kindness.

—Pat Mottola

Displaced

Mama Kabul

Oh, mother city
city of love and mercy
how long must you carry this sorrow,
this pain in your chest.
Daily they kill your citizens.
How broken
your heart is with sorrow,
how large your grief.
Oh, my poor city,
brutality goes on and on,
death, murder in your streets,
you witness the genocide of your children.
I smell fresh blood all over you,
feel your pain in my bones.
Your green dress is now red.
Your happy face is a dream that's faded away.
All I can do for you is pray,
asking God for a better destiny.

Impossible Desire

I want to be born again,
in a place where there is peace.
I want to be born again where I can live more simply,
where I know the route for my life—
where I am able to laugh and be excited
to ride a bicycle in the road
in the rain.

I want to be born again,
and live like a bird, fly over the blue sky
free from every bond.
I want to be a singer
shouting my pain out of my heart.
I want to be a painter with a paintbrush in my hand,
painting the oldest tree of the city,
or a rainbow after rain.

I want to be a poet
disappearing in the world of words,
or in the village with a small garden
and a gray cat lying under sun.

I was born in the shadow of war and
I will die in the shadow of war.

Guardian Angel

Mother, your face is a shining star.
You lighten my darkest nights,
you are rain in the driest deserts.
In my saddest times,
your smile makes me delight.
Pure love holds its nest in your heart.
No doubt you are my guardian angel.
No matter how old I am
you care, help and guide me.
When I am away, your prayer is my protector.
Mother, your kindness is endless
as the green of pine tree,
as the of blueness of the Pacific Ocean,
the height of Hindu Kush Mountain.
Mother, let me kiss your hands;
they are bouquets of beautiful flowers.
Mother, paradise is beneath your feet.
No doubt you are my guardian angel.
Your large black eyes, full of hope,
give me courage in my hardest times.
You are my source of relief
at a time of disappointment
when I fail to reach my goal.
Mother, pat my head to rouse my frozen soul.
Let me admit to this belief:
No one loves me as you do.
No one else accepts me with all my faults.
When I am denied, Mother,
you embrace me, Guardian Angel.
I apologize for the times I caused your tears.

Revolt

Why do you walk two steps ahead of me?
I am more powerful than you.
Do you know why?
Because I have been suffering for centuries.

I am the patient stone against all your cruelty.
When you shout, I say nothing.
When you beat me, I keep silent.
You burn my face, you cut my ears.
You rape me and stone me.

Still I keep quiet.
Do you know why?
Because I am strong!

You exercise your physical power over me
because you have no power of logic.
My calm is not my weakness—
it is the silence of the mighty ocean.

With all my patience I call on you.
I call on you now:
Stop abusing me, stop violating my rights!
Once I revolt,
you will face your real rival.
Be aware of my power. Be afraid of my anger.

Pens and Patience

Pages of history tell women's sad story.
We are the sufferers, the prisoners.
We are forced to be covered, we are stoned to death.
We are sold, we are bought, we are owned,
as private property.
We are forced to die, attacked with acid while walking
if we refuse a marriage.
When our voices rise for justice,
we are kidnapped or shot.
Aggression meets our demand for equality.
Annals of time, beware!
We are women but not powerless, as you think.
We are women but not thoughtless, as you assume.
Our patience is our strength.
Don't consider our humble condition our weakness.
We will wash away from the black
pages of this country all the pains of yesterday.
Singing, we will sign our names on the heart of history!

Kabul

An early Saturday morning,
once again
Mother Kabul is in mourning.
Her heart shattered by terror.
Her sorrowful skirt
is painted with the blood
of hundreds of her innocent children.
Tears in her eyes.
Her shaky body collapsed from pain.
No, no, no—
don't console her!
Let her get her rest.
She has no more patience
for your condolences.
Put your hands on your hearts,
pray for Kabul, pray for Kabul!

I Am Farkhunda

Farkhunda Malikzada, a 27-year old woman falsely accused of burning the Quran, was publicly lynched by a mob in Kabul on March 19, 2015.

When I close my eyes,
I feel what you felt when you were beaten.
I feel the ache of every stone on my head,
cold blood on my face.
I cannot breathe.
I see everything in red.
The faces of murderers are red, the street, the weather, the soil is red.
I dream I am a teacher
    in front of a black board
    explaining something to students.
I dream I am at home
    together with my family
    eating lunch.
Then everything is dark, dark like night.
I lose consciousness, the aches decrease,
    the sounds disappear.
Just one question echoes: what was my sin?
There is a big gap in my heart.

Rest in peace, dear Farkhunda,
released from this cruel society.
They never understand a woman's feelings.
You flew like an angel.
We remain with the murderers.

Beast

for the victims of the war in Ukraine

With dreadful paws
war pounded on our doors
to steal our peace,
bombs pelting like angry rain
spreading death
in our beautiful cities.
With brute force, no compassion,
we were forced to leave our warm beds.

> War has no mercy.
> War has no morals.
> War is brutal!

Hunting our dreams,
evil of all times,
war, stormed in!

Hugging our kids,
shedding tears
out of fear
with thousands of others like us,
we waited in queues for trains
to take us to safety,
leaving our entire life behind,
ready to walk into the unknown.

> War has no mercy.
> War has no morals.
> War is brutal!

Displaced

If you are a displaced person
>   Then you have a sad story.

If you left your roots somewhere behind
>   Then you have wrinkles in your heart.

If you still have images of places you can never see again
>   Then you left an eye behind.

If you walked miles and are unable to return
>   Then you buried hopes deep inside.

If your heart deflates during evenings
>   Then you lost a sense of belonging.

If you speak your language only in your dreams
>   Then you grow a great pain of missing inside.

If your eyes sink deeply
>   Then you miss familiar faces.

If your brain tries to escape a past
>   Then you have already lost a fight.

Rootless

in honor of Syrian refugees

How hard is being rootless?
How far is your dream land?
You call it "Journey of Hope,"
I call it Lost in Darkness.

You walk day and night restless.
My sister, my brother, my friend,
your pain is unbearable,
your dream is huge.
I feel your bleeding heart,
I can read your complex thoughts.

You walk despite your fears.
You walk through fire, gambling your life.
Beautiful children's eyes shedding tears,
each drop puts fire in our hearts.

I pray for God—all that I can do—
to rain showers of peace on your exhausted land.
Perhaps it will extinguish the fire of bombs.
I pray for God to plant love and mercy
in the brutal hearts of mankind.

Cold in Ankara

The big city still in a deep sleep.
To find my way to the main road,
street lights are the only help.
The morning cold slaps my cheeks
as I rush to catch the bus.
The main road is almost empty.
Wearing many layers, I feel heavy.

Few half-awake people accompany me in the bus.
Ah, and the cold never leaves me alone,
I feel it in all my bones.
The only way to avoid this cruel cold is to let my thoughts fly,
take me away from now to other times.
But as if my mind has frozen, my thoughts stick on *cold*.
I think of those living in a tent, without enough warm clothes,
lacking a warm bed. Their sorrow
is deeper, larger than this cold.
This thought hurts more than cold does.
For a minute or two, I control my thinking.
As the bus passes by,
my eyes try to count the lights of each building.
I lose focus, my thinking flows again.
Barefoot children, homeless orphans sleeping on streets...
Painful hearts, lost sense of belonging, lost every belonging...
How do they deal with this cold?
In the middle of nowhere,
only one small flame of hope that keeps them warm.

I say to myself again, *Why do I feel so cold?*
when there are people who feel pain.
Feel unhappy

lost.
detached
lonely
Feel invisible in another land.

Why should cold be a big issue for me,
when others have huge losses?
Blood boils in my heart, pulses through all my veins.
My soul feels the heat
even as my body shakes from head to toe.

The Movement of Clouds

in honor of all refugees

In the twilight of winter evenings,
dozens of white-gray clouds
move slowly from side to side.
Their flowing motion
like thousands of people migrating,
from country to country.

No! I am wrong!
Clouds are not just like people,
but like dreams, hopes...
broken hearts, souls and tired bodies
journeying to an uncertain future.

Half remain in their homeland,
carrying the other half,
like thousands of particles, hopelessly moving
towards sunshine in foreign lands.

Like autumn leaves,
they spend years clinging to life.
Ahh their children, growing like wild plants,
belonging to no country, longing to fit in somewhere...

Let us lend our hands to their hands,
spread hope and smiles to their heartland...
this is what I dream while
looking up at the movement of clouds.

Occupation

Afghanistan under the Taliban's first occupation, 1996-2001

Once upon a time there was a land
with a blue sky and green ground.
Every morning
the sun greeted the land with warmth.
Every evening
the moon and stars lit the dark night.
Flowers colored the pathways.
Birds chirped joyful sounds.
People lived with comfort and joy.
Children played with toys,
girls went to school as did the boys.

It was a timeless autumn day—
the sky darkened.
People worried it was not a good sign.
The sound of the wind was so loud,
the sun disappeared.
Soon, the people learned
a monster had come to occupy the land!

He broke everything,
crumbling their world into sand,
making color disappear from nature—
black and white dominated every feature.
There were no sounds, no light.
There was violence, persecution, horror.
Women were locked inside.
Men were beaten, killed.
Children forgot how to laugh.

But violence cannot stay forever.
Eventually, clouds scattered.
People saw the sun shining again.

Nightmare

Taliban gains control of Afghanistan for the second time in August of 2021

The monsters are back!
Holding their guns,
they take over my green land.
Once again,
for my nation, the nightmare returns.
Evils of time invade my beautiful town.
Enemies of womankind,
ready to attack, like huge black spiders
trapping women and girls inside their webs,
preparing to drain our blood.

Forgotten Land

during Afghanistan's second occupation
by the Taliban, August 2021

We live in a forgotten land.
Dozens of people die every day,
thousands scream from pain.
But their voices don't have sound.

Even the word "death" doesn't translate.
Murder of thousands of Afghans, killed in vain,
as if the color of their blood is not red,
or their wounds have never bled.

All the world bears witness, yet
refuses to hear
refuses to see or understand.

They condemn the violence
but no one is willing to do what it takes
to end the violence in our country.

Deserted by the Sun

When I think of the days you shone on me,
how happy I was to be in a small house,
happy to run off sometimes,
walk to school, see friends,
sing a song or dance.
Without your glow
my happiness is gone.
I can't find my loved ones.
I am left in the bleak land of storms.
I am forgotten in the cold and dark,
waiting for the kind face of the sun,
waiting to shake hands with its light—
the light that takes away the pain.
I want back my green land.
Where are you, Sun?
Bring back the mercy and love
that thrives in your warmth.
Bring back my family,
my mother's love, my father's hands.

Obstacles

She doesn't remember what time it was
but knows it has been a while.
She looks to her watch but it's of no use.
Watches don't show the right time.
She walks in the dark, freezing to death,
thinks it's either too early or too late.
Like an empty hall
echoing her own thought,
she is trapped, lost
between real and unreal,
coexistence or nonexistence.

She carries the heart of a lion,
full of ambition and desire.
Yet,
she is tangled in obstacles
like chains around her neck
to stop her wild spirit.

A poor girl tries to figure out
what's next, struggling to see the right path.
What can be colder than a meaningless dream?
She yearns for warmth in her sunless, suffering country.

I am Not an Object

You cannot own me.
I am a woman
created with strengths—
love, mercy, patience, creativity,
abundance and so much more.
I have deep feelings—
passion, desire,
grief and sadness.
I am not an object.

I am more fragile than a flower,
stronger than diamonds.
My heart is big.
There is room for forgiveness, revenge,
hatred and happiness.
My dreams are large.
I want my basic rights of education and respect.
I work hard.
I am not what you expect
but I am the one I want to be:
the best version of myself!

I enjoy laughter and deep conversations,
questioning life, death, earth, and the universe.
I am not here to take orders
or obey your rules!
You cannot shut me up
or cage me at home!

I have been kept down, reached the depths
of disappointment and despair.

I can sink and rise again
because pain makes me stronger.

Incapable of understanding me,
you insult me, beat me, put me down.
You are afraid of my power.
You cannot own me
because I am not an object.
I am a woman of strength.

Hope

When you come to me,
bring a pair of eyes
so that I can see the world differently.

When you come to me,
bring a bundle of smiles
so that I can feel happiness once again.

When you come to me,
bring a piece of the sun
to light the depths of me
so that I can hold onto life.

Echoes

In Limbo

My soul is tired and aged,
struggling without gain,
in limbo.
Sometimes
I break down into a hundred pieces
only to come together once again.
Sometimes
I don't know where I am—
here, there, everywhere, nowhere.
Sometimes
while out searching for myself
in the chaos of my mind,
I sink into an ocean of thoughts—
present, past, and future swirling,
a question echoing in my ear:
Who am I, who am I?
Uncertain, confused, and lifeless,
without light.
I am nothing more than a picture of black and white.

Lost Piece

Am I borrowed from the future?
Or inherited from the past?
Failing to hold onto the present,
where is my homeland, where is home?
Everywhere fog, dust.
My laughter is all domestic
while I cry in a foreign accent.
That is not me!
That couldn't be me.
To be free from all discontent
there should be a lost piece
here, there, somewhere.
I am going to lock my injured heart
in a small black wooden box
to protect it from more pain.
I'll hang up my passion in the wardrobe,
unused like worn out clothes.
Yet my missing piece, soon or late,
will be found to make me complete.

Technology

My nephew at age three
asked his mom: *Where is my dad?*
She turned her face away,
wiped burning tears
and said, *He became an angel
and moved to heaven.*
My little innocent one
held the smart phone
and said: *Let's call him!*

Mirage

the pain of an early miscarriage

I walk hand in hand with hope.
Heart filled with love and faith.
Mind full of mercy and gratitude.
I walk a long path,
lips repeating prayers,
eyes shedding tears.
I walk with patience—
each step I put forward
leaves prints of strength
and I repeat "you are there"
child of my future, child I carry.
The feeling of joy rises
as I get closer to the dream.

Suddenly,

I find myself in the middle of
an endless barren desert.
Wherever I reach there is nothing—
a mere mirage!
a fatal illusion!
burning sun, sand and dust.
Faith and hope disappear,
leaving behind an empty heart,
a brain filled with clouds.
Eyes stare aimlessly at emptiness.
Feet lose power to move.
The purpose lost, the wishes fly.
Icy heat burns the bones
and leaves behind a handful of ash,
a jar of emptiness.

Expectations

She expects the sun to shine.
She even expects it to smile.
She expects the sea to wave.
She even expects it to dance.
She expects the rain to wash the dust.
She even expects it to sing a song.
She expects the flowers to smell sweet.
She even expects them to talk.
But, she hesitates to expect
goodness from human beings
whose acts of kindness are random
and always questionable.

The Answer

When we pass by
we forget to smile.
We act as blind, deaf and mute.
Is it killing to say hi?
I cry. Have you ever thought why?
Not for a human.
Not for a man.
But for humanity,
which has left us.

Charade

I mourn in silence.
The funeral is inside my head.
My eyes shed dry tears,
my heart shatters.

I mourn in silence.
I mourn inside
for a lost piece of mine,
a lost peace of mind.

I mourn in silence.
People think I am happy
when I wear the fakest smile,
pretending I am alive.

Wild Heart

Between life and death
there is only a narrow line.
So, don't waste your time.
Tame your wild heart with love,
the essence of our being
that guides the motion of the universe,
spreads the seeds of beauty and tranquility
as long as we are alive.

Dialogue

If you tell me life is a battlefield,
>   I tell you fight it hard.
If you tell me you are fatigued,
>   I tell you take a break and then go forward.
If you tell me you want to give up,
>   I tell you breathe and move on.
If you tell me all around you is dark,
>   I tell you the sun will rise soon.
If you tell me your feelings are dead,
>   I tell you your heart is still alive.
If you tell me life doesn't excite you,
>   I tell you excitement is all around you.
If you tell me you are held captive by the chains of life,
>   I tell you to find the strength to cast them off.
If you tell me you want freedom for your soul,
>   I tell you, you must break out!

Write

Let me write about something small,
drops of water over blades of grass.
Or let me write about something colossal,
sunrise, a red fiery
circle on the heart of a blue sky.
Feeling its kind warmth gives me joy.
Or something beautiful,
friendship growing as snowflakes
gathered on the bosom of snow,
covering loneliness.
Oh, I am all mixed up.
Take my pen and paper away,
lock my mind and make me rest.
Let me relax—I don't want to write.
The drops will disappear when the weather warms,
the sun will go away when clouds come,
the friendship will be over when we hurt each other.

Release

Sorrow made its nest in my soul
and then, yes, failure became my shadow
stealing my dreams
blocking my goals.
Caught in the limbo of uncertainty,
swimming in the ocean of hopelessness,
I dangle back and forth aimlessly.
My pain is profound, too deep to be healed.

Faith and hope left me
to anguish daily.
My body is fatigued,
my wounded heart is bleeding,
my pale eyes weep for this miserable destiny,
a cruel and bitter life
devouring me gradually.
My last request, my kind God:
Please send the angel of death
to release this injured soul.

Anguish

If my cries reach the sky,
the blue will shatter
into thousands of pieces.
If the sun could feel
the fire in my heart,
it would be extinguished
from shame.
But God is so patient!
God is so patient!

Negative

They told me:
Stop being so negative!
I counted all positives in my life
and then added the negative ones.
The result came out negative!

Dream Tree

I am tired of dreams
too heavy to carry,

the one about hope.
the one about peace.
the one about love.

I have no more strength
to hold them in my heart.

I will plant my dreams
in the middle of a green park
where random people will often walk
holding hands.

There my dreams will rest,
send deep roots into the earth,
then reach for the sky.

They will grow into a tree
with strong branches of hope,
radiant leaves of passion,
the smell of love in its flowers,
and the silence of peace
in its wide shadow.

Anyone passing by can sit
under the dream tree.
In this quiet space
their wounds will heal.

Echoes

I have been lost
in timeless narrow streets of the past
while I was searching for myself
in the highway of the future.

The present is a high-speed train
moving quickly toward an unknown direction—
life, friendship, love, dreams, happiness...

What a great theatre performance,
everything singing the same song
like the tick-tick-tock of the clock
Be strong!
Be strong!
Be strong!

I want to shout to the mountains
I pass by
I don't want to be strong!
I want to be normal!

But the mountains still echo
Be strong!

Don't Be Afraid

Love in Exile

My heart is a coward.
When it is struck
my hands shake
my tongue stutters
my face fades away.

My heart an empty cage.
I have no courage to open
its broken door.
I lost the key of trust.

When my heart is battered
I sneak under a shell
close my eyes and weep.
I remember how it was young
happy and open.

Now, love is in exile.
Love is prohibited.
Love is expelled
from this fragile cage.
Now, anxiety, sorrow, hatred and fear
live within me.

First Love in Afghanistan

Your name is like a flower
that blooms on the first day of Spring.

A shining star at the heart of blue sky,
it gives light on the darkest winter night.
Your name, the sweetest song the birds sing.
My innocent thoughts compel me
to write your name on my hands,
on papers, notebooks, books,
on my table.
But no!
I must keep it out of sight.

The Invisible Wall

The wall between us is so thick
we cannot see each other
we cannot hear each other.

This cultural wall is so strong
we cannot break it down.
This wall is protected by others,
law makers of the society.

The wall between us is so tall
it hides you from me and me from you.
My hands cannot reach you.

The wall grows bigger and bigger.
My sorrow grows deeper and deeper.
I want to see you, feel you.
I want to touch you, smell you.

As the wall expands, my heart bursts.
I fear this invisible wall
intends to keep us apart.

Salty Kiss

The sea and the sky were blue.
They merged as one
while you and I submerged in chilly water
drunk on the wine of love.

I remember how you hugged my body
to your chest,
held me tight from my waist
in lover's embrace
inside the blue sea.
The taste of your salty kiss
still remains in my lips.

Seasons

to my husband

I never knew
where you were.
I never guessed
when and how you would arrive.
But I always believed
that you existed under this vast uncertain sky.

You came at the perfect time.
You gave me happiness as a gift,
brought back my smiles, cleared off my fears,
swept away my tears.

Before you
I was drowned in an ocean of sadness,
frozen in the land of ice,
forgotten in a loveless country.
My days and nights were gray.

You shined on me, brought me the gleam of sun,
healed my insecurity.
You brought color into my life.
I see the ground green and the sky blue.

Now that you are here at the right time,
please don't go.

If you do,
again, I will be dull and cold,
lose you and lose my faith.
My heart will be back to prison to fade.
I will be left as a withered tree.

Winter Nights

In the long winter nights
when snow covers the surface of earth,
when nothing moves from dead cold,
even wind stops motion.
But rockets and bombs
hover around to haunt lives,
lighting the night.
Their sounds vibrate in my ears.

When you are away
I stay awake till midnight
hoping to see you again,
my eyes afraid to close.
Fears appear like ghosts
when I fall asleep without you.

The noise in my head gets louder,
the shadows start chasing me,
the darkness gets deeper.
Pages of my life turn one by one
mixing up my past, present and future.
When endless war persists
my profound fear increases.

In this cold bed, my only desire:
If only you stayed with me
I would have your kind and warm hands
to hold mine so tight
and stay awake next to me,
wait until I fall asleep,
and keep away my bad dreams.

Longing

You are gone for days.
I am left waiting.

Only repeating your name
gives me the power to breathe.
Missing you each second
hurts my soul.

Sometimes, even with you,
I feel lonely.
Grab my hand, tell me a story,

the story in which we have
two kids and a puppy,
live in a small cottage away
from crowds and noise,
stroll in our own yard with few worries.

Ghost

Invisible pain, a stain
of love on my heart.
First heartfelt smile,
first time you held my hand,
said I was your life.
We promised to die
together, remember?

You were a lie, a ghost, a dream.
Did you hear about the girl
who cries every night?
Did you hear she lost her mind?

Miracle

for my son

Happiness knocked on my door
and my sorrows went away
when you came into the world.

Our eyes connected,
I fell in love with you.
You were love itself—
    love even
    beyond love.
So innocent and pure.
When you put your small hands in my hands
you melt my heart.
With you, I have witnessed to firsts:
    a first smile,
    a first word,
    a first step.

You are the secret of my happiness
    the light of my eyes,
    my heartbeat,
    my breath.

Don't Be Afraid

My little divine miracle,
don't be afraid, live happily!
Hold my hand tightly.
Keep your feet steady.

I will raise you with poems
so you can walk over the clouds
and catch your highest dreams.

I will raise you with love
so you can see beauty in the universe
with the eyes of your heart.

I will feed your soul with music
so you can understand the language of flowers
and talk to the birds.

Don't be afraid, live happily!

November

For my son's birthday

I have fallen in love with November
With its foggy mornings
With its rainy weathers
With its sly breezes
And with its every colorful leaf.
I have fallen in love with November
Because November gifted you to me
And I was reborn!

Gone

on the death of a husband

You divided into two:
a part of you in the ground
a part of you in the heaven.
I am in a desert of disappointment
with an ocean of grief inside me.
You left the world like wind
carrying away the colors of my soul.
And you left me
with uncompleted dreams.

Departure

I am leaving tonight
carrying a huge bag of memory
with a fragile and frozen heart.
For the last time, look at my eyes.
As a last word, say you love me.
I am leaving tonight.

Trees

When hope is packing to move
you need to find a way.

When it is too hard to stay silent,
shout as loud as you can on the rocks
or to an empty well.
When you feel nothing can stop your tears,
weep deeply but know that on a rainy day
rain washes your tears away.

If you have no one to talk to,
if you feel lonely,
choose a tree, but an old one.
Sit next to it and talk
>   about all sad stories
>   about your regrets
>   about your fears
>   about your broken heart
>   about your stolen dreams
>   about your dead soul
>   about fake promises
>   and anything that crushes your heart.

The tree will listen patiently.
And at the end of the day
"It is you who must answer to yourself."

Maybe I Should Fly

I don't belong here.

I want to fly back where I came from.
I want to go around the earth,
find the spot where I belong
and live simply.

I want to fly where birds sing their sweetest songs,
where I can hear waterfowl, where it is green all the time,
where flowers smile and butterflies speak.

I want to fly where I can write poems and sing songs,
where dancing is not forbidden.

I want to fly where people are happy, where children don't cry,
where memories don't die.
I want to be free to laugh.

I want to fly up to the deep sky.
I want to be free from evil eyes.
I want to be free from captivity.
I want to fly and live simply
where love is not denied.

About the Authors

The Labib sisters were born into an enlightened family in Kabul, Afghanistan. Farida Labib has a PhD in International Relations and Shafiqa Labib has a Master's degree in Political Science. They grew up in Afghanistan during civil war and the Taliban period, witnessing violations against Afghan women and deprivation of their basic human rights, such as the right to education. Both sisters write poetry and short stories in Farsi, Turkish, and English. Their experiences during war, and of being women in Afghanistan, a country which largely denies them freedom of expression, impacts their work. *Maybe I Should Fly* is their first collection of poetry in the English language.

Acknowledgments

We are grateful to *Afghanvoices.meidum.com* and to *Afghan Women's Writing Project*, where many of these poems, sometimes in slightly different forms or with different titles, were originally published.

We offer our gratitude also to Patricia Mottola, whose encouragement and editorial advice led to the publication of this book.

We will wash away from the black pages of this country all the pains of yesterday.

www.ingramcontent.com/pod-product-compliance
Lightning Source LLC
Chambersburg PA
CBHW060351130626
46553CB00003B/1175